FACILITATOR'S GUIDE

Creating and Protecting the Shared Foundation

of a Professional Learning Community at Work™

Richard DuFour
Rebecca DuFour
Tim Brown
Mike Mattos

Solution Tree | Press

a division of Solution Tree

555 North Morton Street
Bloomington, IN 47404
800.733.6786 (toll free) / 812.336.7700
FAX: 812.336.7790
email: info@SolutionTree.com
SolutionTree.com

Visit **go.SolutionTree.com/PLCbooks** to download the free reproducibles in this book.

Printed in the United States of America

FSC
www.fsc.org
MIX
From responsible sources
FSC® C016529

Solution Tree
Jeffrey C. Jones, CEO
Edmund M. Ackerman, President

Solution Tree Press
President: Douglas M. Rife
Editorial Director: Tonya Maddox Cupp
Managing Production Editor: Caroline Weiss
Senior Production Editor: Suzanne Kraszewski
Senior Editor: Amy Rubenstein
Media Editor: Peggie Howard
Copy Chief: Sarah Payne-Mills
Copy Editor: Miranda Addonizio
Proofreader: Elisabeth Abrams
Cover and Text Designer: Rian Anderson

Facilitator's Guide Writer: Jackson Moore

Table of Contents

Reproducible pages are in italics.

Notes to the Facilitator

This workshop is for educators who are attempting to implement the professional learning community (PLC) process, as well as those who hope to strengthen their existing PLCs. Its purpose is to provide educators with greater clarity about the process and the importance of aligning practices, policies, and procedures with the shared foundation of effective PLCs. The workshop is intended to instill a deeper understanding of the assumptions and thought processes of PLC members and to supply the compelling rationale behind *why* educators should fully commit to the PLC process.

Using the four pillars of the PLC foundation, the workshop presents opportunities for personal reflection and group collaboration leading to:

- The construction and implementation of a school's mission, vision, values (collective commitments), and goals
- Use of tools to help establish and align practices and procedures with the PLC foundation
- A means by which school professionals can identify and address discrepancies between practice and pledges

This workshop is based on the work of Richard DuFour, Rebecca DuFour, Robert Eaker, Thomas W. Many, and Mike Mattos (2016) and influenced by the writings of Kerry Patterson and colleagues, authors of *Crucial Conversations: Tools for Talking When Stakes Are High* (Patterson, Grenny, McMillan, & Switzler, 2002), and Joseph Grenny and colleagues, authors of *Influencer: The New Science of Leading Change* (Grenny, Patterson, Maxfield, McMillan, & Switzler, 2013). The workshop is divided into eight components.

1. **Welcome and Opening:** This segment establishes the context in which members of a true PLC think. It explores how the journey to PLC success begins with the four pillars of the PLC foundation.
2. **The Mission Pillar—Establishing a Mission for Your School:** This segment defines a mission statement, identifies the biggest problems schools have with mission statements, and presents research in support of establishing a mission statement. Importantly, it also introduces "The Professional Learning Communities at Work™ Continuum: Laying the Foundation," a tool to help school staff members build shared knowledge.
3. **The Vision Pillar—Establishing a Vision Statement for Your School:** This segment explains the vision statement and provides the opportunity for participants to evaluate and create a vision statement that impacts their daily practice.
4. **The Values Pillar—Establishing a Values Statement (Collective Commitments) for Your School:** This segment asks participants to develop the PLC mindset by clarifying the commitments they

are willing to make to help create the school described in their shared vision. This pillar is the most frequently overlooked pillar in the PLC foundation, and yet it is vital to the PLC process because it moves people from discussion to action.

5. **The Goals Pillar—Establishing Goals for Your School:** This segment presents the importance of goals that are specific and strategic, measurable, attainable, results oriented, and time bound (SMART) in the PLC process, asking participants to write a team SMART goal that aligns to a school improvement goal. Participants then share their perceptions on which, if any, of the four pillars of the foundation warrant additional attention.
6. **Clarifying Your Current Reality Pertaining to the PLC Foundation:** In this segment, participants actively begin building background information about their schools through the use of the "A Data Picture of Our School" instrument.
7. **Aligning Practices and Processes With the PLC Foundation:** Participants evaluate a role-play segment in which a principal and members of a collaborative team discuss traditional grading practices in the context of the school's foundation. This segment asks participants to identify and discuss one practice in their school that seems misaligned with a commitment to high levels of learning for all students.
8. **Addressing Discrepancies Between Actual Practice and the Pledges of the Foundation and Closing:** Finally, participants have the opportunity to consider whether or not their own school should address behaviors and practices that are clearly inconsistent with the purposes and priorities established in the PLC foundation. They learn strategies to *influence up*—that is, to help persuade the principal to take steps to protect and strengthen the PLC foundation.

Conducting the Workshop

The workshop is designed to be either a full-day experience or two half-day sessions. This set includes all of the professional development materials you will need, including a video (approximately forty-seven minutes) featuring insight and instruction from Richard DuFour and Rebecca DuFour, overhead masters, several worksheets, and group discussion handouts. All are intended to engage participants in serious reflection and dialogue about conditions in their own schools. Participants receive time for lunch and breaks.

To conduct a successful learning event, please consider the following.

- **Preparation:** Please view the entire video program, read all materials, and complete all activities.
- **Location:** The workshop should take place in an area large enough for individual, team, and whole-group work.
- **Equipment:** You will need a DVD player, a projector, and one or more monitors. Ideally, you will have one video monitor for every ten to twelve participants. You may also create transparencies of the handouts and display them with an overhead projector or computer projector.

- **Handouts:** This guide includes reproducible handouts for all participants (starting on page 25). Duplicate these handouts before the workshop begins and distribute them to participants according to the workshop instructions.

- **Additional equipment:** You will need note paper and pens for each participant. Flip charts, whiteboards, or chalkboards and appropriate writing materials are useful for group discussions.

- **Refreshments:** The agenda for the workshop should include one or more breaks in which beverages are on hand. Snacks and lunch are optional, but water should be available throughout the session.

Video Program

This workshop incorporates a video program that is approximately forty-seven minutes in length. The video begins with an introduction by Richard DuFour of the four pillars of the PLC foundation and continues with instruction by both Richard and Rebecca DuFour to help educators construct a mission statement, a vision statement, collective commitments, and goals. Each of the four pillars is presented in "The Professional Learning Communities at Work™ Continuum: Laying the Foundation" (divided into four separate tools—Shared Mission, Shared Vision, Collective Commitments [Shared Values], and Shared Goals)—and "The Professional Learning Communities at Work™ Continuum: Using School Improvement Goals to Drive Team Goals." These documents, along with the team-reflection tool "A Data Picture of Our School," form the basis for workshop activities. Your workshop handouts include all of these documents.

Print

Learning by Doing: A Handbook for Professional Learning Communities at Work™, Third Edition by Richard DuFour, Rebecca DuFour, Robert Eaker, Thomas W. Many, and Mike Mattos

Crucial Conversations: Tools for Talking When Stakes Are High, Second Edition by Kerry Patterson, Joseph Grenny, Ron McMillan, and Al Switzler

Influencer: The New Science of Leading Change, Second Edition by Joseph Grenny, Kerry Patterson, David Maxfield, Ron McMillan, and Al Switzler

Video

Leading Difficult Conversations: Professional Learning Communities at Work™: Professional development video set by Richard DuFour and Rebecca DuFour

Web

allthingsplc.info

go.SolutionTree.com/PLCbooks

Workshop Overview at a Glance

Time (in Minutes)	Section	Handouts and Overheads
20	Welcome and Opening	Learning Objectives
50	The Mission Pillar	Why Should We Clarify Our Mission? Four Questions About Our Mission Statement The Professional Learning Communities at Work™ Continuum: Laying the Foundation—Shared Mission
45	The Vision Pillar	Why Should We Describe the School or District We Are Trying to Create? Five Questions About Our Vision Statement The Professional Learning Communities at Work™ Continuum: Laying the Foundation—Shared Vision
45	The Values Pillar (Collective Commitments)	Why Should We Articulate Collective Commitments? Three Questions About Our Values Statement (Collective Commitments) The Professional Learning Communities at Work™ Continuum: Laying the Foundation—Collective Commitments (Shared Values)
45	The Goals Pillar	Why Do We Need SMART Goals? Five Questions About Our Goals The Professional Learning Communities at Work™ Continuum: Using School Improvement Goals to Drive Team Goals The Professional Learning Communities at Work™ Continuum: Laying the Foundation—Shared Goals The Four Pillars of a PLC Foundation
45	Clarifying Your Current Reality Pertaining to the PLC Foundation	The Foundation of Anywhere High School A Data Picture of Our School

continued →

60	Aligning Practices and Processes With the PLC Foundation	Criteria for Evaluation of Role-Play Video Segment Discussion Questions for After the Role-Play Segment on Standards-Based Grading
30	Addressing Discrepancies Between Actual Practice and the Pledges of the Foundation and Closing	Why Should School Leaders Address Practices? Influencing Up: How Teacher Leaders Can Encourage Principals to Lead the PLC Process More Effectively

Workshop Steps and Teaching Suggestions: Statement of Purpose

The purpose of this workshop is to provide members of a professional learning community with greater clarity about the PLC process, the foundation that supports this process, and the importance of aligning practices, policies, and procedures with that foundation.

Learning Objectives

After viewing the video and participating in the activities for the workshop, participants will be able to:

- Demonstrate the need for a solid foundation in a PLC
- Clarify the various elements of a solid PLC foundation
- Assess their school's PLC foundation
- Demonstrate how to conduct a difficult conversation when a traditional practice does not align with the commitments presented in the PLC foundation
- Help identify conflicts or practices in their school that are misaligned with the PLC process so that they can address them
- Stress the importance of confronting practices, procedures, and behaviors that are not aligned with the PLC foundation
- Offer suggestions for teacher leaders on how to influence up

Program Overview

This video program presents the four foundational pillars necessary to build a successful PLC. It presents opportunities for personal reflection and group collaboration leading to:

- The creation and implementation of a school's mission, vision, values (collective commitments), and goals

- Use of tools pertaining to establishing and aligning practices and procedures with the PLC foundation
- The means by which school professionals can address discrepancies between practice and commitments

Materials

- **Video program:** *Creating and Protecting the Shared Foundation of a Professional Learning Community at Work™*
- **Overhead masters:**
    - Learning Objectives
    - Four Questions About Our Mission Statement
    - Five Questions About Our Vision Statement
    - Three Questions About Our Values Statement (Collective Commitments)
    - Five Questions About Our Goals
    - The Four Pillars of a PLC Foundation
    - Criteria for Evaluation of Role-Play Video Segment
- **Handout masters:**
    - Why Should We Clarify Our Mission?
    - The Professional Learning Communities at Work™ Continuum: Laying the Foundation—Shared Mission
    - Why Should We Describe the School or District We Are Trying to Create?
    - The Professional Learning Communities at Work™ Continuum: Laying the Foundation—Shared Vision
    - Why Should We Articulate Collective Commitments?
    - The Professional Learning Communities at Work™ Continuum: Laying the Foundation—Collective Commitments (Shared Values)
    - Why Do We Need SMART Goals?
    - The Professional Learning Communities at Work™ Continuum: Using School Improvement Goals to Drive Team Goals
    - The Professional Learning Communities at Work™ Continuum: Laying the Foundation—Shared Goals
    - The Foundation of Anywhere High School
    - A Data Picture of Our School

    - Discussion Questions for After the Role-Play Segment on Standards-Based Grading
    - Why Should School Leaders Address Practices?
    - Influencing Up: How Teacher Leaders Can Encourage Principals to Lead the PLC Process More Effectively
- Flip charts, chalkboards, or whiteboards with appropriate writing materials

Activities

It is best to follow the activities as outlined in the workshop teaching suggestions and pause the video when prompted. After showing each segment of the video program, allow participants time to comment, express opinions, or ask questions about the material. If requested, you can replay portions of the program as participants consider the questions and activities.

Welcome and Opening

1. Welcome participants to the workshop and introduce yourself and anyone else serving as workshop host, coleader, or organizer.
2. If participants do not know one another well, conduct a "getting to know you" activity. Ask participants to form pairs and interview each other for a few minutes. Then ask the pairs to introduce each other to the group, stating the other person's name, something interesting about that person, and what he or she hopes to gain from the workshop. (If there are more than twenty people in the group, have each pair join another pair and make introductions only within each group of four.)
3. Using the overhead master "Learning Objectives," briefly review the objectives of the workshop.
4. Ask the participants to take a moment to consider their own mindsets regarding the PLC process, even if they are just beginning implementation. Encourage them to jot down privately a sentence or phrase expressing how they feel about the PLC process as it currently functions in their schools. Then tell them to put the notes away as you will return to them at the end of the program.
5. Start the video. A "Pause for Group Work" title card will prompt you when to stop.

Note: The video references chapter 2 in the book *Learning by Doing: A Handbook for Professional Learning Communities at Work™, Third Edition*, by Richard DuFour, Rebecca DuFour, Robert Eaker, Thomas W. Many, and Mike Mattos (2016).

The Mission Pillar—Establishing a Mission for Your School

1. Refer participants to the handout titled "Why Should We Clarify Our Mission?" Allow a few minutes for participants to review this sampling of research conclusions that leading educational scholars have reached.
2. Ask participants to cite the mission statement of their school. If all are from the same school, you can write this on a flip chart, whiteboard, chalkboard, display it on an alternate projector, or show a

handout you prepared before the session. If participants are from multiple schools, you can ask for and record samples.

3. Using the overhead master "Four Questions About Our Mission Statement," conduct a group discussion in which participants answer the following questions. Appoint someone to act as group recorder.

   - Does our mission statement reflect a commitment to high levels of learning for all students?
   - Do the members of our faculty know the mission statement of our school or district?
   - Can we provide examples of practices in our school that align with our mission statement?
   - Can we cite examples of practices in our school that do not align with our mission statement?

   Note: If your group is bigger than twenty individuals, break into smaller discussion groups and assign discussion leaders and recorders who will report back to the main group.

4. Return to the video and continue until prompted with the "Pause for Group Work" title card.
5. Distribute the handout "The Professional Learning Communities at Work™ Continuum: Laying the Foundation—Shared Mission," ask participants to consider the descriptions of the five stages of the PLC continuum for the mission pillar of a PLC and then, individually, silently, and honestly assess the current status of their school for the mission pillar.
6. Establish small groups of four or more members and have participants share their findings.
7. Poll each group on the mission pillar. Is there general agreement or wide disparity?
8. Finally, lead a group discussion regarding steps that they could take to create a more effective mission statement for their school. Appoint a recorder to keep notes on the flip chart and then post the responses.

Suggested fifteen-minute break

After the break, return to the video and play the segment "The Vision Pillar." Continue until prompted with the next "Pause for Group Work" title card.

The Vision Pillar—Establishing a Vision Statement for Your School

1. Distribute the handout "Why Should We Describe the School or District We Are Trying to Create?" Ask participants to take a few minutes to review these research statements from leading educators.
2. Break into small discussion groups and have participants share their thoughts about this research. Ask a reporter from each group to deliver group conclusions.
3. Using the overhead master "Five Questions About Our Vision Statement," lead a discussion of the following questions. Some will elicit immediate consensus; others may spark debate. Appoint a recorder and post your results.

   - Do we have a shared vision of the school we hope to become?

- Did the faculty play a major role in developing the vision statement?
- Does the faculty know the vision statement?
- Does the vision statement focus primarily on what others—students, parents, administrators, central office personnel, the community, the board of education, the state legislature—can do to improve the school, or does it focus on what educators can do?
- What specific steps can we point to that we have taken to move our school toward its stated vision?

4. Return to the video and continue until the next "Pause for Group Work" title card.
5. When you have completed this group work, ask participants to turn to the handout "The Professional Learning Communities at Work™ Continuum: Laying the Foundation—Shared Vision."
6. Establish small groups of four or more members and have participants share their findings.
7. Poll each group on the vision pillar. Is there general agreement or wide disparity?
8. Lead a group discussion with participants regarding steps they can take to create a more effective vision statement for their school. Appoint a recorder to keep notes on the flip chart and then post the responses.
9. Return to the video and play the segment "The Values Pillar." Continue until prompted with the "Pause for Group Work" title card.

The Values Pillar—Establishing a Values Statement (Collective Commitments) for Your School

1. Ask each participant to write a commitment sentence for his or her role in the PLC that will support the vision of his or her collaborative team in order to take responsibility for student achievement. This sentence should begin with phrases like "I promise to . . ." or "We commit to . . . ."
2. Ask volunteers to share commitments and encourage others to expand them into collective commitments the collaborative teams can share. Share a few of your own sentences to start and sustain the discussion.
3. Distribute the handout "Why Should We Articulate Collective Commitments?" and ask participants to take a few minutes to review these research data.
4. Return to the video and continue until the next "Pause for Group Work" title card.
5. Using the overhead master "Three Questions About Our Values Statement (Collective Commitments)," lead a group discussion of the following questions.
   - Has our faculty clarified the specific collective commitments we have made in order to advance the vision of our school so we can better achieve its fundamental purpose?
   - Are these commitments stated as actions and behaviors rather than beliefs?
   - Once again, do the commitments have an internal focus (what *we* will do) or an external focus (what *others* must do)?

6. Return to the video and continue until the next "Pause for Group Work" title card.
7. Ask participants to turn to the handout "The Professional Learning Communities at Work™ Continuum: Laying the Foundation—Collective Commitments (Shared Values)."
8. Then establish small groups of four or more members and have participants share their findings.
9. Poll each group on the values pillar. Is there general agreement or wide disparity?
10. Lead a group discussion regarding steps participants can take to create a more effective vision statement for their school. Appoint a recorder to keep notes on the flip chart and then post the responses.
11. Use this last pause before lunch to review the five stages on the continuum for the PLC shared mission, shared vision, and collective commitments pillars. Ask participants if they have any questions about establishing and implementing these collective commitments.

Suggested lunch break

The Goals Pillar—Establishing Goals for Your School

1. After the lunch break, distribute the handout "Why Do We Need SMART Goals?" which is a sampling of research on writing goals that are strategic and specific, measurable, attainable, results oriented, and time bound. Give participants a few minutes to read it over.
2. Return to the video and play the segment "The Goals Pillar." Continue until prompted by the next "Pause for Group Work" title card.
3. Using the overhead "Five Questions About Our Goals," ask the group to consider the following questions.
   - Do we have improvement goals for our school this year?
   - Do all members of the faculty know the goals our school is pursuing?
   - Are the school's goals reflected in the goals of each of our grade-level or course-specific teams?
   - Are our team's goals SMART goals?
   - Can you write a SMART goal?
4. Distribute the handout "The Professional Learning Communities at Work™ Continuum: Using School Improvement Goals to Drive Team Goals," which explains the importance of SMART goals in the PLC process, as well as examples and nonexamples of SMART goals.
5. Ask each participant to write a SMART goal that his or her course- or grade-level PLC team could use immediately. Then divide participants into small groups of three to four members and have them share the goals they've written. After a few minutes, bring the group together and ask for volunteers to share examples. Ask the group to determine whether or not the stated goals are SMART.
6. Ask participants to turn to the handout "The Professional Learning Communities at Work™ Continuum: Laying the Foundation—Shared Goals."

7. Then establish small groups of four or more members and have participants share their findings.
8. Poll each group on the goals pillar. Is there general agreement or wide disparity?
9. Display the overhead master "The Four Pillars of a PLC Foundation."
10. Return to the video and continue until the next "Pause for Group Work" title card.

Clarifying Your Current Reality Pertaining to the PLC Foundation

1. Distribute the handout "The Foundation of Anywhere High School." Take a few moments to evaluate this model and compare it to your own school's foundation.
2. Distribute the three-page handout "A Data Picture of Our School," which provides a template that participants can use to build background information about their schools. Ask the participants to take a few minutes to review the blank template and fill in any boxes for which they feel they know the answer (there may not be many).
3. Present participants with "A Data Picture of Our School" that you have researched and completed in advance of the workshop. Discuss any surprises.
4. If participants are not all from the same school, you could present a completed data picture form from a school, ask participants to review it, and see if there are any questions or curiosities that arise from any of the data.

Note: Encourage participants to reference *Learning by Doing, Third Edition* (DuFour et al., 2016), for a thorough review of the most promising practices in school improvement and the overwhelming research base supporting them.

Suggested fifteen-minute break

After the break, return to the video and continue until the next "Pause for Group Work" title card.

Aligning Practices and Processes With the PLC Foundation

1. Before viewing the role-play video segment, use the overhead master "Criteria for Evaluation of Role-Play Video Segment" and review the following checklist. As you watch the role-play segment on standards-based grading, ask yourself how the principal:
   - Engages in inquiry in an attempt to clarify the team's rationale for its practice
   - Seeks common ground and points of agreement
   - Uses the foundation to support the need for re-examining practice
   - Seeks to build shared knowledge regarding alternative practices
2. Return to the video and the role-playing segment. Continue until the next "Pause for Role-Play Discussion" title card.

After the Role-Play Segment

1. Distribute the handout "Discussion Questions for After the Role-Play Segment on Standards-Based Grading." Divide participants into small groups. Ask groups to discuss the team meeting they just observed using the following questions.
   - How did the principal raise the issue for discussion?
   - Does the principal question the motives or integrity of the teachers?
   - What are examples of the principal attempting to engage in collective inquiry by asking the team to provide a rationale for its practices?
   - What are examples of the principal seeking to establish common ground?
   - What are examples of how the principal uses the school's shared foundation in this dialogue?
   - Give examples of how the principal used the shared foundation in this dialogue.
   - What are the strategies the principal proposed for building shared knowledge about alternative practices?
   - This video segment focused on the issue of what a grade represents. Is there a clear understanding and consistent action on this question in our school?
   - Is it fair to students if their teachers in the same course or grade level use widely divergent criteria in determining their grades?
   - Can you cite an example of a traditional practice in our school that may not align with a commitment to helping all students learn at high levels?
   - We have frequently been told that principals are unwilling to initiate this kind of dialogue. Why do you think this is the case?
   - Assuming the faculty has reached consensus on the pillars of the shared foundation, do you think it is important that a principal addresses practices or behaviors that are clearly inconsistent with the pillars? Why or why not?
2. After several minutes, have the full group reconvene and lead a discussion on responses to the video segment. Ensure that you give attention to the discussion question in which participants identify an example of nonalignment to commitment within their own teams.
3. Return to the video and continue until the "Pause for Discussion on PLCs and School Improvement" title card.

Note: If time permits, you can review the handout and the evaluation cues, then replay the role-play video segment a second time to reinforce the modeling procedure. This role-play segment begins at approximately 29:32 on the video time stamp.

You can also use the video segment and appropriate handouts at a later time in a team follow-up session.

Joining Richard and Rebecca DuFour in the roleplay are Solution Tree authors Tim Brown and Mike Mattos.

Addressing Discrepancies Between Actual Practice and the Pledges of the Foundation and Closing

1. Distribute the handout "Why Should School Leaders Address Practices?" and allow participants a few minutes to review.
2. Distribute the handout "Influencing Up: How Teacher Leaders Can Encourage Principals to Lead the PLC Process More Effectively."
3. Lead a group discussion of the two handouts focusing on PLCs and school improvement. Ask participants why they think principals might be reluctant to raise the issue of discrepancies between actual practice and the pledges of the foundation.
4. Ask participants to review the initial notes they made at the opening of the workshop regarding their perceptions of PLCs. Ask them to consider these two questions.
    a. Do you believe it is desirable for a faculty to have a shared sense of purpose, vision, collective commitments, and SMART goals?
    b. Do you feel it is feasible for your faculty to create a shared foundation that could be beneficial to your school?
5. Return to the video, where you will see the "In Closing" title card, and play the remainder of the video.

Overhead Masters

Learning Objectives

After viewing the video and participating in the activities for the workshop, participants will be able to:

- *Demonstrate the need for a solid foundation in a PLC*
- *Clarify the various elements of a solid PLC foundation*
- *Assess their school's PLC foundation*
- *Demonstrate how to conduct a difficult conversation when a traditional practice does not align with the pledges presented in the PLC foundation*
- *Help identify conflicts or practices in their school that are misaligned with the PLC process and that they should address*
- *Stress the importance of responding to practices, procedures, and behaviors that are not aligned with the PLC foundation*
- *Offer suggestions to teacher leaders on how they can influence up*

Four Questions About Our Mission Statement

1. Does our mission statement reflect a commitment to high levels of learning for all students?
2. Do the members of our faculty know the mission statement of our school or district?
3. Can we provide examples of practices in our school that align with that mission statement?
4. Can we cite examples of practices in our school that do not align with our mission statement?

Five Questions About Our Vision Statement

1. Do we have a shared vision of the school we hope to become?
2. Did the faculty play a major role in developing the vision statement?
3. Does the faculty know the vision statement?
4. Does the vision statement focus primarily on what others—students, parents, administrators, central office personnel, the community, the board of education, the state legislature—can do to improve the school, or does it focus on what educators can do?
5. What specific steps can we point to that we have taken to move our school toward its stated vision?

Three Questions About Our Values Statement (Collective Commitments)

1. Has our faculty clarified the specific collective commitments we have made in order to advance the vision of our school so we can better achieve its fundamental purpose?
2. Are these commitments stated as actions and behaviors rather than beliefs?
3. Once again, do the commitments have an internal focus (what *we* will do) or an external focus (what *others* must do)?

Five Questions About Our Goals

1. Do we have improvement goals for our school this year?
2. Do all members of the faculty know the goals our school is pursuing?
3. Are the school's goals reflected in the goals of each of our grade-level or course-specific teams?
4. Are our team's goals SMART goals?
5. Can you write a SMART goal?

The Four Pillars of a PLC Foundation

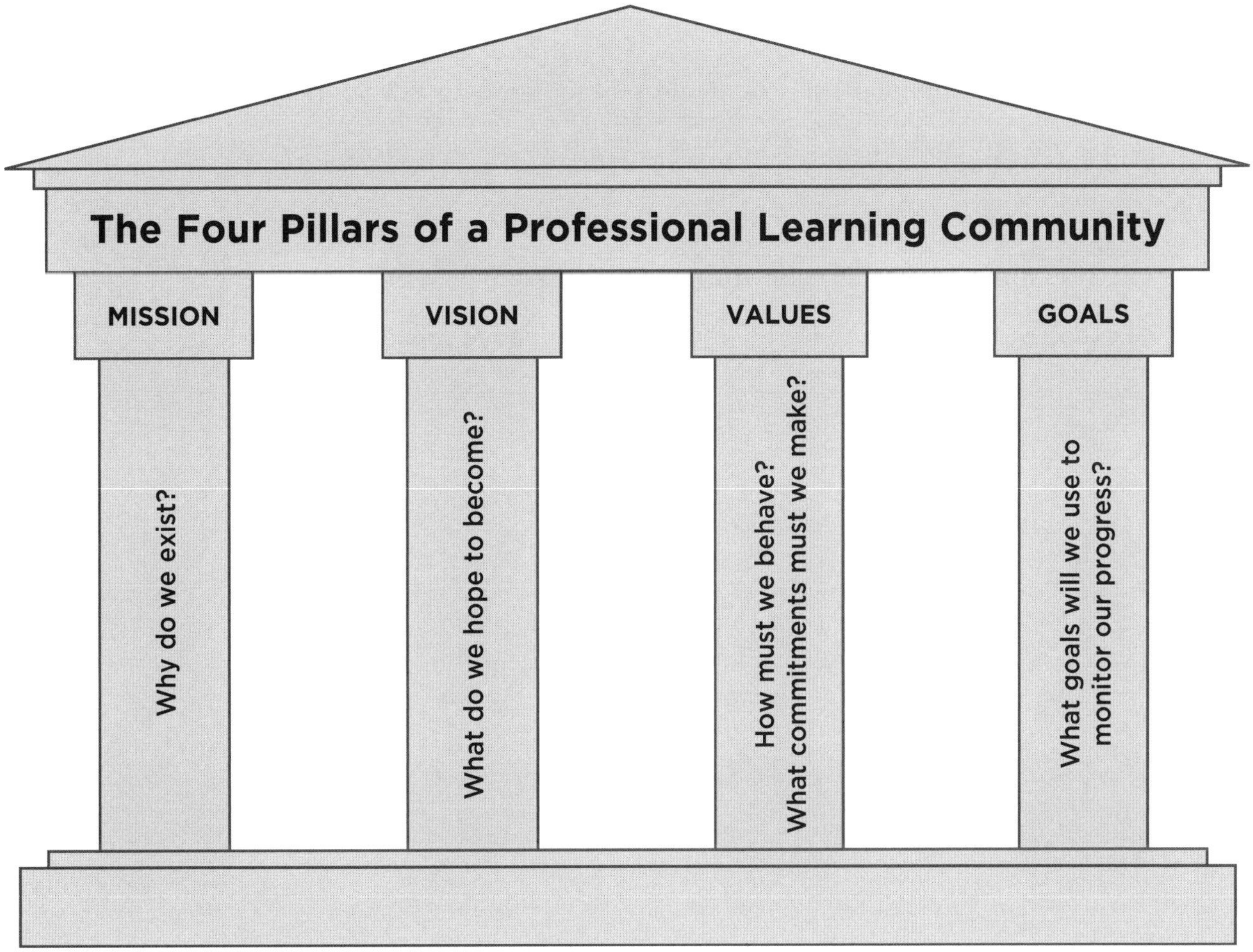

Criteria for Evaluation of Role-Play Video Segment

As you watch the role-play segment on standards-based grading, ask yourself how the principal:

1. Engages in inquiry in an attempt to clarify the team's rationale for its practice
2. Seeks common ground and points of agreement
3. Uses the foundation to support the need for re-examining practice
4. Seeks to build shared knowledge regarding alternative practices

Handout Masters

Why Should We Clarify Our Mission?

"There is no point in thinking about changes in structure until the school achieves reasonable consensus about its intellectual mission for children" (Newmann & Wehlage, 1996, p. 295).

"Members of great organizations think they are 'on a mission from God. . . . [They] always believe that they are doing something vital, even holy . . . something worthy of their best selves. . . . Their clear collective purpose makes everything they do seem meaningful and valuable'" (Bennis & Biederman, 1997, p. 204).

"In the effective school, there is a clearly articulated mission of the school through which the staff shares an understanding of and a commitment to the school's goals, priorities, assessment procedures, and accountability. . . . The issue of mission is one that must receive substantial discussion" (Lezotte, 2002, pp. 4–5).

"Contrary to popular wisdom, the proper first response to a changing world is NOT to ask, 'How should we change,' but rather, 'What do we stand for and why do we exist?' This should never change. And then feel free to change everything else. Put another way, visionary companies distinguish between their core values and enduring purpose (which should never change) from their operating practices and business strategies (which should be changing constantly in response to an ever-changing world)" (Collins & Porras, 1994, p. xiv).

The Wallace Foundation study of effective district leadership found that district offices that had a positive influence on schools and student achievement established clear purpose that was widely shared (Leithwood et al., 2009).

"The most deeply motivated people—not to mention those that are most productive and satisfied—hitch their desires to a cause larger than themselves. . . . Nothing bonds a team like a shared mission. The more people that share a common cause . . . the more your group will do deeply satisfying and outstanding work" (Pink, 2011, pp. 131, 174).

Research examining successful schools reveals that they share the characteristics of modern high-performance workplaces that foster cultures built on teamwork and shared mission (Anrig, 2013).

A "persuasive and valuable" mission statement "gives people a context for their" actions and empowers them "to support one another's efforts" and fully engage their talents and imagination (Halvorson, 2014, p. 38).

"Leaders need the ability to develop a shared moral purpose and meaning as well as a pathway for attaining that purpose. . . . Great leaders connect others to the reasons they became educators—their moral purpose" (Fullan & Quinn, 2016, p. 17).

Educators who believe that merely clarifying or reaffirming their mission will somehow improve results are certain to be disappointed. In fact, in many schools, developing a mission statement has served as a substitute, rather than a catalyst, for meaningful action. Merely drafting a new mission statement does not automatically change how people act, and therefore writing a mission statement does nothing to close the knowing-doing gap (Pfeffer & Sutton, 2000).

The Professional Learning Communities at Work™ Continuum: Laying the Foundation—Shared Mission

DIRECTIONS: Individually, silently, and *honestly* assess the current reality of your school's implementation of each indicator listed in the left column. Consider what evidence or anecdotes support your assessment. This form may also be used to assess district or team implementation.

We have a clear sense of our collective purpose, the school we are attempting to create to achieve that purpose, the commitments we must make and honor to become that school, and the specific goals that will help monitor our progress.

Indicator	Pre-Initiating	Initiating	Implementing	Developing	Sustaining
Shared Mission It is evident that learning for all is our core purpose.	The purpose of the school has not been articulated. Most staff members view the mission of the school as teaching. They operate from the assumption that although all students should have the opportunity to learn, responsibility for learning belongs to the individual student and will be determined by his or her ability and effort.	An attempt has been made to clarify the purpose of the school through the development of a formal mission statement. Few people were involved in its creation. It does little to impact professional practice or the assumptions behind those practices.	A process has been initiated to provide greater focus and clarity regarding the mission of learning for all. Steps are being taken to clarify what, specifically, students are to learn and to monitor their learning. Some teachers are concerned that these efforts will deprive them of academic freedom.	Teachers are beginning to see evidence of the benefits of clearly established expectations for student learning and systematic processes to monitor student learning. They are becoming more analytical in assessing the evidence of student learning and are looking for ways to become more effective in assessing student learning and providing instruction to enhance student learning.	Staff members are committed to helping all students learn. They demonstrate that commitment by working collaboratively to clarify what students are to learn in each unit, creating frequent common formative assessments to monitor each student's learning on an ongoing basis, and implementing a systematic plan of intervention when students experience difficulty. They are willing to examine all practices and procedures in light of their impact on learning.

Why Should We Describe the School or District We Are Trying to Create?

"At both school and district levels, administrative tasks essential to teachers' learning and learning communities include building a shared vision and common language about practice" (McLaughlin & Talbert, 2006, p. 80).

"The very best leaders understand that their key task is inspiring a *shared* vision, not selling their own idiosyncratic view of the world" (Kouzes & Posner, 2006, p. 108).

"A vision builds trust, collaboration, interdependence, motivation, and mutual responsibility for success. Vision helps people make smart choices, because their decisions are made with the end result in mind. . . . Vision allows us to act from a proactive stance, moving toward what we want. . . . Vision empowers and excites us to reach for what we truly desire" (Blanchard, 2007, p. 22).

In order for a school to move forward its faculty needs to develop an understood and agreed-on purpose and sense of direction. "If you don't have a common, agreed-upon destination, then everyone is left to his or her own devices to imagine one—a scenario that results in unharnessed and unfocused efforts" (Gabriel & Farmer, 2009, p. 46).

A key responsibility of an educational leader is "developing and delivering a compelling picture of the school's future that produces energy, passion, and action in yourself and others. . . . [A vision is] one of your most potent leadership tools for the development of coherent and sustainable actions" (Kanold, 2011, pp. 6–7).

In identifying five key functions of principals, the Wallace Foundation (2012) listed shaping a vision of academic success as the first of those functions. It concludes, "Effective principals are responsible for establishing a schoolwide vision of commitment to high standards and the success of all students" (p. 5).

"Shared vision emerges from a collaboratively defined understanding of what constitutes worthwhile student learning, with all members of the PLC working together on problems around that common vision" (Fulton & Britton, 2011, p. 14).

A powerful vision results in inspiration, aspiration, and perspiration. It inspires people to rally round a greater purpose. It challenges educators to articulate the school they aspire to create. It leads to action, beginning with building shared knowledge of what it will take to reduce the gap between the current reality of their school and the school described in the vision (Williams & Hierck, 2015).

"The better people can envision where they are going, the more they can focus on specific initiatives that will make that vision a reality" (Kotter International, 2015, p. 17).

Shared vision emerges when there is clarity of purpose and "continuous collaborative conversations that build shared language, knowledge, and expectations" (Fullan & Quinn, 2016, p. 29).

The Professional Learning Communities at Work™ Continuum: Laying the Foundation—Shared Vision

DIRECTIONS: Individually, silently, and *honestly* assess the current reality of your school's implementation of each indicator listed in the left column. Consider what evidence or anecdotes support your assessment. This form may also be used to assess district or team implementation.

We have a clear sense of our collective purpose, the school we are attempting to create to achieve that purpose, the commitments we must make and honor to become that school, and the specific goals that will help monitor our progress.

Indicator	Pre-Initiating	Initiating	Implementing	Developing	Sustaining
Shared Vision We have a shared understanding of and commitment to the school we are attempting to create.	No effort has been made to engage staff in describing the preferred conditions for the school.	A formal vision statement has been created for the school, but most staff members are unaware of it.	Staff members have participated in a process to clarify the school they are trying to create, and leadership calls attention to the resulting vision statement on a regular basis. Many staff members question the relevance of the vision statement, and their behavior is generally unaffected by it.	Staff members have worked together to describe the school they are trying to create. They have endorsed this general description and use it to guide their school improvement efforts and their professional development.	Staff members can and do routinely articulate the major principles of the school's shared vision and use those principles to guide their day-to-day efforts and decisions. They honestly assess the current reality in their school and continually seek more effective strategies for reducing the discrepancy between that reality and the school they are working to create.

Why Should We Articulate Collective Commitments?

With the democratization of organizations, especially schools, the leadership function becomes one of creating a "community of shared values" (Lezotte, 1991, p. 3).

"Values describe how we intend to operate, on a day-to-day basis, as we pursue our vision. . . . Values are best expressed in terms of behavior: If we act as we should, what would an observer see us doing? . . . If values are made a central part of the organization's shared vision effort, and put out in full view, they become like a figurehead on a ship: a guiding symbol of the behavior that will help move people toward the vision" (Senge et al., 1994, p. 302).

Both profit and nonprofit organizations should be grounded on "a timeless set of core values and an enduring purpose" (Collins & Porras, 1994, p. xxiv).

"The language of complaint essentially tells us, and others, what it is we can't stand. The language of commitment tells us (and possibly others) what it is we stand for" (Kegan & Lahey, 2001, p. 32).

High-performing districts "tended to rely more on a common culture of values to shape collective action than on bureaucratic rules and controls. The shared values typically focused on improvement of student learning as the central goal" (Elmore, 2000, p. 26).

"Values provide guidelines on how you should proceed as you pursue your purpose and picture of the future. They answer the question . . . 'How?' They need to be clearly described so that you know exactly what behaviors demonstrate that the value is being lived" (Blanchard, 2007, p. 30).

Values must be driven into the policy, the decision-making, and ultimately the culture of the organization, otherwise value statements are just words. When values become part of an employee's DNA, they not only guide day-to-day work but also empower employees to act in unique situations (Berry & Seltman, 2008).

"Values represent the *commitments to action* necessary to ensure the vision is realized. . . . In the best PLC cultures, vision and values ultimately become the driving force behind the decision-making process that takes place every day" (Kanold, 2011, p. 13).

To bring a mission statement to life "educators must be willing to transparently communicate their commitment to students as it relates to their stated mission and challenge one another to live up to that commitment" (Muhammad & Hollie, 2012, p. 28).

The key to values impacting the organization in a positive way is that people have to "live by them, reinforce them every day, and not tolerate behavior that is at odds with them" (Bryant, 2014).

The Professional Learning Communities at Work™ Continuum: Laying the Foundation—Collective Commitments (Shared Values)

DIRECTIONS: Individually, silently, and *honestly* assess the current reality of your school's implementation of each indicator listed in the left column. Consider what evidence or anecdotes support your assessment. This form may also be used to assess district or team implementation.

We have a clear sense of our collective purpose, the school we are attempting to create to achieve that purpose, the commitments we must make and honor to become that school, and the specific goals that will help monitor our progress.

Indicator	Pre-Initiating	Initiating	Implementing	Developing	Sustaining
Collective Commitments (Shared Values) We have made commitments to each other regarding how we must behave in order to achieve our shared vision.	Staff members have not yet articulated the attitudes, behaviors, or commitments they are prepared to demonstrate in order to advance the mission of learning for all and the vision of what the school might become.	Administrators or a committee of teachers have created statements of beliefs regarding the school's purpose and its direction. Staff members have reviewed and reacted to those statements. Initial drafts have been amended based on staff feedback. There is no attempt to translate the beliefs into the specific commitments or behaviors that staff will model.	A statement has been developed that articulates the specific commitments staff have been asked to embrace to help the school fulfill its purpose and move closer to its vision. The commitments are stated as behaviors rather than beliefs. Many staff object to specifying these commitments and prefer to focus on what other groups must do to improve the school.	Staff members have been engaged in the process to articulate the collective commitments that will advance the school toward its vision. They endorse the commitments and seek ways to bring them to life in the school.	The collective commitments are embraced by staff, embedded in the school's culture, and evident to observers of the school. They help define the school and what it stands for. Examples of the commitments are shared in stories and celebrations, and people are challenged when they behave in ways that are inconsistent with the collective commitments.

Why Do We Need SMART Goals?

"According to research, goal setting is the single most powerful motivational tool in a leader's toolkit. Why? Because goal setting operates in ways that provide purpose, challenge, and meaning. Goals are the guideposts along the road that make a compelling vision come alive. Goals energize people. Specific, clear, challenging goals lead to greater effort and achievement than easy or vague goals do" (Blanchard, 2007, p. 150).

"Goal setting is one of the simplest and most effective organizational interventions that can be used to increase employee performance" (O'Hora & Maglieri, 2006, p. 132).

"[Schools with teachers who learn and students who achieve] use clear, agreed-upon student achievement goals to focus and shape teacher learning" (WestEd, 2000, p. 12).

"Collegial support and professional development in schools are unlikely to have any effect on improvement of practice and performance if they are not connected to a coherent set of goals that give direction and meaning to learning and collegiality" (Elmore, 2003, p. 60).

California elementary schools that outperformed schools with similar student populations assigned a high priority to student achievement, set measurable goals for improved student achievement, and had a well-defined plan to improve achievement (Williams et al., 2005).

"Consistently higher performing high schools set explicit academic goals that are aligned with and often exceed state standards" (Dolejs, 2006, p. 1).

"Our investigations suggest it is critical to define and publish a protocol that articulates specific inquiry functions: jointly and recursively identifying appropriate and worthwhile goals for student learning; finding or developing appropriate means to assess student progress toward those goals; bringing to the table the expertise of colleagues and others who can assist in accomplishing these goals; planning, preparing, and delivering lessons; using evidence from the classroom to evaluate instruction; and, finally, reflecting on the process to determine next steps" (Gallimore et al., 2009, pp. 548–549).

"One of the greatest challenges to team success is the inattention to results. . . . But there is no getting around the fact that the only measure of a great team—or a great organization—is whether it accomplishes what it sets out to accomplish. . . . When it comes to how a cohesive team measures its performance, one criterion sets it apart from noncohesive ones: its goals are shared across the entire team" (Lencioni, 2012, pp. 65–66).

Schools that have the greatest impact on student learning establish clear and measurable goals focused on improving overall student achievement at the school level. "Data are analyzed, interpreted, and used to regularly monitor progress toward student achievement goals" (Marzano, Warrick, & Simms, 2014, p. 57).

"The problem is not the absence of goals in districts and schools today but the presence of too many that are ad hoc, unconnected, and ever-changing. . . . [They are too often fragmented and so] people see them as discrete demands with little or no connection to . . . their daily work. . . . The solution lies in developing limited goals, persisting, and avoiding distractors. . . . These leaders . . . [use goals] to establish continuous focused direction" (Fullan & Quinn, 2016, pp. 20–21).

The Professional Learning Communities at Work™ Continuum: Using School Improvement Goals to Drive Team Goals

DIRECTIONS: Individually, silently, and *honestly* assess the current reality of your school's implementation of each indicator listed in the left column. Consider what evidence or anecdotes support your assessment. This form may also be used to assess district or team implementation.

We assess our effectiveness on the basis of results rather than intentions.

Indicator	Pre-Initiating	Initiating	Implementing	Developing	Sustaining
The members of each of our collaborative teams are working interdependently to achieve one or more SMART goals that align with our school goals. Each team has identified specific action steps members will take to achieve the goal and a process for monitoring progress toward the goal. The identification and pursuit of SMART goals by each collaborative team are critical elements of the school's continuous improvement process.	Goals have not been established at the district or school level. Teams are not expected to establish goals.	Teams establish goals that focus on adult activities and projects rather than student learning.	Teams have been asked to create SMART goals, but many teachers are wary of establishing goals based on improved student learning. Some attempt to articulate very narrow goals that can be accomplished despite students learning less. Others present goals that are impossible to monitor. Still others continue to offer goals based on teacher projects. There is still confusion regarding the nature of and reasons for SMART goals.	All teams have established annual SMART goals as an essential element of their collaborative team process. Teams have established processes to monitor their progress, and members work together in an effort to identify strategies for becoming more effective at achieving the team's SMART goal.	Each collaborative team of teachers has established both an annual SMART goal and a series of short-term goals to monitor their progress. They create specific action plans to achieve the goals, clarify the evidence that they will gather to assess their progress, and work together interdependently to achieve the goal. This focus on tangible evidence of results guides the work of teams and is critical to the continuous improvement process of the school. The recognition and celebration of efforts to achieve goals help sustain the improvement process.

page 1 of 2

Where Do We Go From Here? Worksheet
Using School Improvement Goals to Drive Team Goals

Indicator of a PLC at Work	What steps or activities must be initiated to create this condition in your school?	Who will be responsible for initiating or sustaining these steps or activities?	What is a realistic timeline for each step or phase of the activity?	What will you use to assess the effectiveness of your initiative?
The members of each of our collaborative teams are working interdependently to achieve one or more SMART goals that align with our school goals. Each team has identified specific action steps members will take to achieve the goal and a process for monitoring progress toward the goal. The identification and pursuit of SMART goals by each collaborative team are critical elements of the school's continuous improvement process.				

The Professional Learning Communities at Work™ Continuum: Laying the Foundation—Shared Goals

DIRECTIONS: Individually, silently, and *honestly* assess the current reality of your school's implementation of each indicator listed in the left column. Consider what evidence or anecdotes support your assessment. This form may also be used to assess district or team implementation.

We have a clear sense of our collective purpose, the school we are attempting to create to achieve that purpose, the commitments we must make and honor to become that school, and the specific goals that will help monitor our progress.

Indicator	Pre-Initiating	Initiating	Implementing	Developing	Sustaining
Common School Goals We have articulated our long-term priorities, short-term targets, and timelines for achieving those targets.	No effort has been made to engage the staff in establishing school improvement goals related to student learning.	Goals for the school have been established by the administration or school improvement team as part of the formal district process for school improvement. Most staff would be unable to articulate a goal that has been established for their school.	Staff members have been made aware of the long-term and short-term goals for the school. Tools and strategies have been developed and implemented to monitor the school's progress toward its goals. Little has been done to translate the school goal into meaningful targets for either collaborative teams or individual teachers.	The school goal has been translated into specific goals that directly impact student achievement for each collaborative team. If teams are successful in achieving their goals, the school will achieve its goal as well. Teams are exploring different strategies for achieving their goals.	All staff members pursue measurable goals that are directly linked to the school's goals as part of their routine responsibilities. Teams work interdependently to achieve common goals for which members are mutually accountable. The celebration of the achievement of goals is part of the school culture and an important element in sustaining the PLC process.

The Foundation of Anywhere High School

Our Mission: To help *all* of our students achieve the high levels of learning required for success in college or post-secondary training

Our Vision: The policies, programs, and practices of Anywhere High School reflect its commitment to helping all students learn at high levels.

As a Result of That Commitment:

- The staff constantly seeks out the most promising practices that support student learning.
- The school is characterized by a collaborative culture in which educators take collective responsibility for helping all students learn at high levels.
- The collaborative team is the fundamental structure of the school.
- Students are provided a guaranteed and viable curriculum, unit by unit.
- The learning of each student is monitored on an ongoing basis through daily formative assessment in the classroom and team-developed common formative assessment for each unit.
- The school has systems in place to ensure that evidence of student learning is used to—
    - Provide timely, diagnostic, and directive support for students who are struggling
    - Enrich and extend learning for students who demonstrate they are highly proficient
    - Inform individual educators regarding their strengths and weaknesses in helping students to learn at high levels
    - Alert a collaborative team to areas of concern in student learning that warrant the attention of the entire team
- The school supports educators' continuous learning and ongoing professional development.
- The school has a strong partnership with parents and provides parents with the information they need to monitor and support the learning of their children.

Our Collective Commitments: In order to fulfill our fundamental purpose and become the school we describe in our vision statement, each member of the staff commits to the following—

- I will be a positive, contributing member of my collaborative team.
- I will teach the essential learnings of our agreed-upon curriculum, unit by unit.
- I will monitor each student's learning on an ongoing basis through classroom and team-developed formative assessments.
- I will use evidence of student learning to inform and improve my practice and to better meet the needs of individual students.
- I will work with my colleagues to achieve our SMART goals.
- I will seek out the most promising practices to support student learning.
- I will keep parents informed of the progress of their children.

Our Schoolwide Goals: We will monitor the following indicators to mark our progress—

- Reduce the failure rate.
- Increase the percentage of students pursuing and being successful in the most rigorous curriculum in each program.
- Increase student achievement on local, state, and national high-stakes assessments.
- Increase the percentage of our graduates who experience success in postsecondary learning.

A Data Picture of Our School

School Name:				
Student Achievement Results				
Indicator	**Year 20__-20__**	**Year 20__-20__**	**Year 20__-20__**	**Facts About Our Data**
Based on Our School Assessment Data				
Based on Our District Assessment Data				
Based on Our State or Provincial Assessment Data				
Based on Our National Assessment Data				
Student Engagement Data				
Average Daily Attendance				
Percentage of Students in Extracurricular Activities				
Percentage of Students Using School's Tutoring Services				
Percentage of Students Enrolled in Most Rigorous Courses Offered				
Percentage of Students Graduating Without Retention				
Percentage of Students Who Drop Out of School				

page 1 of 3

Student Engagement Data (continued)				
Indicator	**Year 20__-20__**	**Year 20__-20__**	**Year 20__-20__**	**Facts About Our Data**
Other Areas in Which We Hope to Engage Students, Such as Community Service				
Discipline				
Number of Referrals / Top Three Reasons for Referrals				
Number of Parent Conferences Regarding Discipline				
Number of In-School Suspensions				
Number of Detentions / Saturday School				
Number of Out-of-School Suspensions				
Number of Expulsions				
Other				
Survey Data				
Student Satisfaction or Perception Assessment				
Alumni Satisfaction or Perception Assessment				
Teacher Satisfaction or Perception Assessment				

page 2 of 3

Survey Data (continued)				
Indicator	**Year 20__-20__**	**Year 20__-20__**	**Year 20__-20__**	**Facts About Our Data**
Administration Satisfaction or Perception Assessment				
Community Satisfaction or Perception Assessment				
Demographic Data				
Percent Free and Reduced Lunch				
Percent Mobility				
Percent Special Education				
Percent English as a Second Language				
Percent White (Not of Hispanic Origin)				
Percent Black				
Percent Hispanic				
Percent Asian				
Percent Native American				

Discussion Questions for After the Role-Play Segment on Standards-Based Grading

- *How did the principal raise the issue for discussion?*
- *Does the principal question the motives or integrity of the teachers?*
- *What are examples of the principal attempting to engage in collective inquiry by asking the team to provide a rationale for its practices?*
- *What are examples of the principal seeking to establish common ground?*
- *Give examples of how the principal uses the school's shared foundation in this dialogue.*
- *What are the strategies the principal proposed for building shared knowledge about alternative practices?*
- *This video segment focused on the issue of what a grade represents. Is there a clear understanding and consistent action on this question in your school?*
- *Is it fair to students if their teachers in the same course or grade level use widely divergent criteria in determining their grades?*
- *Can you cite an example of a traditional practice in your school that may not align with a commitment to helping all students learn at high levels?*
- *We have frequently been told that principals are unwilling to initiate this kind of dialogue. Why do you think this is the case?*
- *Assuming the faculty has reached consensus on the pillars of the shared foundation, do you think it is important that a principal address practices or behaviors that are clearly inconsistent with the pillars? Why or why not?*

Why Should School Leaders Address Practices?

School leaders should address practices and behaviors that are clearly inconsistent with the purpose and priorities established in a school's mission, vision, collective commitments, and goals. And here's why.

- *Failure to address practices and behaviors that are clearly inconsistent with the stated purpose and priorities sends the message to the entire faculty that the practice or behavior is acceptable and gives others permission to replicate it.*
- *The lack of congruence between stated purpose and priorities and actual practice and behavior weakens and breeds cynicism about the PLC process.*
- *An important component in the PLC process is mutual trust. School leaders whose behavior reflects a school's purpose and priorities build trust. Leaders whose actions are not aligned with the stated purpose and priorities erode faculty trust.*
- *If the practices and behavior of some individuals and teams do not reflect the PLC process, those teachers deny their students the full benefit of the PLC process.*

Influencing Up: How Teacher Leaders Can Encourage Principals to Lead the PLC Process More Effectively

Below, we offer specific strategies a team of teacher leaders might use to encourage their principal to take more assertive steps for advancing the school's PLC journey. In this case, although the school's mission statement pledges a commitment to help all students learn at high levels, and the vision statement promises students who experience difficulty will receive additional time and support for learning, the school has done nothing systematic to provide such time and support. The team schedules a meeting with the principal to discuss the matter. Before the meeting they consider the following tips and frame their dialogue accordingly.

1. Assume good intentions on the principal's part. Chances are the principal comes to work each day hoping to do a good job.
2. Clarify up front in the dialogue what you want and don't want to result from the conversation.

   "We want to brainstorm some ideas with you about strengthening the PLC process in our school. We don't want you to think that we are being critical of or are attempting to usurp your leadership. We simply see a problem in advancing our PLC process, and we know that you are essential to finding solutions."
3. Seek mutual purpose and common ground.

   "We know that, like us, you sincerely want this school to be a great place for both student and adult learning, a school we can all be proud of. Like you, we would be excited if our school could become the kind of place described in our vision statement."
4. Be concise when presenting the problem and as factual as possible.

   "We think one of the barriers that has hampered our PLC journey is the lack of a systematic process to provide students with additional time and support for learning. It is left up to each teacher to resolve. This seems contrary to our commitments to support high levels of learning for all *students and to take* collective *responsibility for that learning. It seems that if all students are to learn, some will need more time and support than others. We think a system to provide that time and support should reflect our collective responsibility rather than a series of individual decisions and actions."*
5. Frame the problem as a gap between expectations and actions.

   "We feel this is a disconnect between the expectations that we created when we established our PLC foundation and the day-to-day work that we experience. If we can address that disconnect successfully, it will demonstrate to the entire staff that our school is genuinely committed to the PLC process. More importantly, we believe it will help more students learn at higher levels and make the work of teachers more manageable."

6. Build shared knowledge.

   "We have brought some research with us for you to review that we think supports the importance of systematic intervention in PLCs. We believe it is compelling and are really interested in your take on it when you have a chance to look it over."

7. Offer tangible assistance in moving forward.

   "We would be happy to develop some alternative schedules that could provide time for intervention for your review. If you conclude a particular schedule has promise, we would also take responsibility for convincing the faculty of the need for that schedule. Finally, if you want to establish a task force to help us use time for systematic intervention most successfully, some of us would be happy to serve on it along with any others you might want to invite.

8. Encourage the principal to share his or her thought process.

   "What is your reaction to our proposal? Are we off base in assuming that if the question of intervention continues to be left to each teacher to resolve, it will be difficult for us to take collective responsibility for higher levels of student learning? How do you feel about creating a schoolwide system of interventions? Do you see problems that we might not have identified?"

9. Ask for a follow-up meeting to discuss progress, problems, or concerns.

   "We know we are proposing a substantive change in our traditional practice and we anticipate you will need some time to think about it and review the research we brought you. Could we schedule a meeting in the next week or two at your convenience to discuss the matter? Is there anything you would like us to do in the meantime to prepare for that meeting?"

page 2 of 2

References

Anrig, G. (2013). *Beyond the education wars: Evidence that collaboration builds effective schools.* New York: Century Foundation Press.

Bennis, W., & Biederman, P. W. (1997). *Organizing genius: The secrets of creative collaboration.* New York: Basic Books.

Berry, L. L., & Seltman, K. D. (2008). *Management lessons from Mayo Clinic: Inside one of the world's most admired service organizations.* New York: McGraw-Hill.

Blanchard, K. (2007). *Leading at a higher level: Blanchard on leadership and creating high performing organizations.* Upper Saddle River, NJ: Prentice Hall.

Bryant, A. (2014, January 4). Management be nimble. *New York Times.* Accessed at www.nytimes.com/2014/01/05/business/management-be-nimble.html?_r=0 on September 10, 2015.

Collins, J., & Porras, J. I. (1994). *Built to last: Successful habits of visionary companies.* New York: HarperBusiness.

Dolejs, C. (2006). *Report on key practices and policies of consistently higher performing high schools.* Washington, DC: National High School Center. Accessed at http://betterhighschools.org/docs/ReportOfKeyPracticesandPolicies_10-31-06.pdf on January 10, 2010.

DuFour, R., & DuFour, R. (2011). *Leading difficult conversations: Professional Learning Communities at Work* [DVD]. Bloomington, IN: Solution Tree Press.

DuFour, R., DuFour, R., Eaker, R., Many, T. W., & Mattos, M. (2016). *Learning by doing: A handbook for Professional Learning Communities at Work* (3rd ed.). Bloomington, IN: Solution Tree Press.

Elmore, R. F. (2000). *Building a new structure for school leadership.* Washington, DC: Albert Shanker Institute. Accessed at http://citeseerx.ist.psu.edu/viewdoc/download?doi=10.1.1.103.7688&rep=rep1&type=pdf on January 20, 2010.

Elmore, R. F. (2003). *Knowing the right thing to do: School improvement and performance-based accountability.* Washington, DC: National Governors Association Center for Best Practices.

Fullan, M., & Quinn, J. (2016). *Coherence: The* right *drivers in action for schools, districts, and systems.* Thousand Oaks, CA: Corwin Press.

Fulton, K., & Britton, T. (2011, June). *STEM teachers in professional learning communities: From good teachers to great teaching.* Washington, DC: National Commission on Teaching and America's Future.

Gabriel, J. G., & Farmer, P. C. (2009). *How to help your school thrive without breaking the bank.* Alexandria, VA: Association for Supervision and Curriculum Development.

Gallimore, R., Ermeling, B. A., Saunders, W. M., & Goldenberg, C. (2009). Moving the learning of teaching closer to practice: Teacher education implications of school-based inquiry teams. *Elementary School Journal, 109*(5), 537–553.

Grenny, J., Patterson, K., Maxfield, D., McMillan, R., & Switzler, A. (2013). *Influencer: The new science of leading change* (2nd ed.). New York: McGraw-Hill.

Halvorson, G. C. (2014). Getting to "us." *Harvard Business Review, 92*(9), 38.

Kanold, T. D. (2011). *The five disciplines of PLC leaders.* Bloomington, IN: Solution Tree Press.

Kegan, R., & Lahey, L. L. (2001). *How the way we talk can change the way we work: Seven languages for transformation.* San Francisco: Jossey-Bass.

Kotter International. (2015). *Eight steps to accelerate change in 2015.* Accessed at www.kotterinternational.com /ebook/Kotter-8-steps-ebook.pdf on January 26, 2016.

Kouzes, J. M., & Posner, B. Z. (2006). *A leader's legacy.* San Francisco: Jossey-Bass.

Leithwood, K., Louis, K. S., Wahlstrom, K., Anderson, S., Mascall, B., Michlin, M., et al. (2009). *Learning from district efforts to improve student achievement.* New York: Wallace Foundation.

Lencioni, P. (2012). *The advantage: Why organizational health trumps everything else in business.* San Francisco: Jossey-Bass.

Lezotte, L. W. (1991). *Correlates of effective schools: The first and second generation.* Okemos, MI: Effective Schools Products. Accessed at www.effectiveschools.com/images/stories/escorrelates.pdf on January 6, 2006.

Lezotte, L. W. (2002). *Revolutionary and evolutionary: The effective schools movement.* Accessed at www .effectiveschools.com/images/stories/RevEv.pdf on January 10, 2010.

Marzano, R. J., Warrick, P., & Simms, J. A. (2014). *A handbook for high reliability schools: The next step in school reform.* Bloomington, IN: Marzano Research.

McLaughlin, M. W., & Talbert, J. E. (2006). *Building school-based teacher learning communities: Professional strategies to improve student achievement.* New York: Teachers College Press.

Muhammad, A., & Hollie, S. (2012). *The will to lead, the skill to teach: Transforming schools at every level.* Bloomington, IN: Solution Tree Press.

Newmann, F. M., & Wehlage, G. G. (1996). Conclusion: Restructuring for authentic student achievement. In F. M. Newmann & Associates (Eds.), *Authentic achievement: Restructuring schools for intellectual quality* (pp. 286–301). San Francisco: Jossey-Bass.

O'Hora, D., & Maglieri, K. A. (2006). Goal statements and goal-directed behavior: A relational frame account of goal setting in organizations. *Journal of Organizational Behavior Management, 26*(1), 131–170.

Patterson, K., Grenny, J., McMillan, R., & Switzler, A. (2002). *Crucial conversations: Tools for talking when stakes are high.* New York: McGraw-Hill.

Pfeffer, J., & Sutton, R. I. (2000). *The knowing-doing gap: How smart companies turn knowledge into action.* Boston: Harvard Business School Press.

Pink, D. H. (2011). *Drive: The surprising truth about what motivates us.* New York: Riverhead Books.

Senge, P., Ross, R., Smith, B., Roberts, C., & Kleiner, A. (1994). *The fifth discipline fieldbook: Strategies and tools for building a learning organization.* New York: Doubleday.

Wallace Foundation. (2012, January). *The school principal as leader: Guiding schools to better teaching and learning.* New York: Author. Accessed at www.wallacefoundation.org/knowledge-center/school-leadership/effective-principal-leadership/Documents/The-School-Principal-as-Leader-Guiding-Schools-to-Better-Teaching-and-Learning.pdf on January 7, 2012.

WestEd. (2000). *Teachers who learn, kids who achieve: A look at schools with model professional development.* San Francisco: Author.

Williams, K. C., & Hierck, T. (2015). *Starting a movement: Building culture from the inside out in professional learning communities.* Bloomington, IN: Solution Tree Press.

Williams, T., Perry, M., Studier, C., Brazil, N., Kirst, M., Haertel, E., et al. (2005). *Similar students, different results: Why do some schools do better?* Mountain View, CA: EdSource.

Learning by Doing, Third Edition
Richard DuFour, Rebecca DuFour, Robert Eaker, Thomas W. Many, and Mike Mattos
Discover how to transform your school or district into a high-performing PLC. The third edition of this comprehensive action guide offers new strategies for addressing critical PLC topics, including hiring and retaining new staff, creating team-developed common formative assessments, and more.
BKF746

Concise Answers to Frequently Asked Questions About Professional Learning Communities at Work™
Mike Mattos, Richard DuFour, Rebecca DuFour, Robert Eaker, and Thomas W. Many
Get all of your PLC questions answered. Designed as a companion resource to *Learning by Doing: A Handbook for Professional Learning Communities at Work (3rd ed.)*, this powerful, quick-reference guidebook is a must-have for teacher teams working to build and sustain a PLC.
BKF705

Leading Difficult Conversations
Featuring Richard DuFour and Rebecca DuFour
Gain strategies for addressing the conflicts that can result from transforming a school into a professional learning community. Learn how to hold conversations that lead staff to understand that best practice is to work collaboratively and collectively in high-performing teams.
DVF047

Professional Learning Communities at Work™ Plan Book
Rebecca DuFour, Richard DuFour, and Robert Eaker
Teachers love this plan book! This great organizer, with 40 weekly planning pages and space for eight class periods, is also a process book packed with creative ideas, activities, and inspirational success stories that address crucial, teacher-specific PLC concepts.
BKF217

Professional Learning Communities at Work™ and Virtual Collaboration
Richard DuFour and Casey Reason
Learn how to combine the capacities of the PLC at Work™ process and powerful technology tools to transform teaching and learning. Realize the potential of virtual collaboration to support the PLC process, and discover research-based strategies for reaching sustained levels of deeper learning.
BKF673